MW01592453

Spiritualjutsu

Mike Lafrance

Copyright © 2020 Mike Lafrance

All rights reserved.

ISBN: 9798668790630

DEDICATION

Crystal, Romeo, Neliah and Lowen. Thanks for being great!

ACKNOWLEDGMENTS

I am so grateful for the amazing instructors and students I had over the 30 years I have practiced martial arts. I did not know it at the time, but you taught me my first gospel lessons long before I met the missionaries.

I am grateful for a loving mother, energetic kids and dependable friends. I wanted to thank Ed Goldthorp who has been a source of pure joy when it comes to learning, loving and living the gospel of Jesus Christ.

Thoughtful conversations are doors to meaningful ideas, and I have had so many of these conversations with such great people. Capturing my experiences and placing them in this book has been hard because I am not a writer. I was able to do this through the help of my oldest son Romeo who was the first person to read the book and not laugh out loud. Also, a big thank you to Maryangel Chapman who at the end of this writing journey took her time and talents to share ideas and thoughts that got me to the finish line.

To my fancy face companion, thank you for being my best friend and providing endless protection that makes me and our children feel safe. Thanks Crystal!

Finally, thank you to a Savior who is not just an infinite God but who is an intimate one. You know my name and always remember me, even when I don't.

INTRODUCTION

This book is based on a few powerful lessons I learned over the years as a martial arts student, instructor and founder of my own ninjutsu system.

As I look back on these lesson's years later, I begin to see some very powerful principles that directly connect to the Gospel of Jesus Christ. I enjoyed connecting my experiences with those from the scriptures and in so doing have been able to respond to these scriptures in ways that have been joyful and spiritually motivating.

Spiritualjutsu is not a new martial art that can be studied at a local dojo but rather a method of techniques that increase our spiritual capacity, or in other words spiritual skills. It's important to understand the breakdown of the words themselves. Look at these word breakdowns:

Ninjutsu

Nin- Endurance, perseverance and Stealth

Jutsu- Method of Technique and Skill

Based on this definition we can see Ninjutsu means that we use specific methods and techniques to develop skills of endurance and perseverance.

Now when we look at Spiritualjutsu:

Spiritualjutsu

Spiritual- Affecting the spirit or soul

Jutsu- Method of Technique and Skill

Based on this definition we can see Spiritualjutsu means that we use specific methods and techniques to develop the skills that will affect our spirits or souls.

My goal is to take you through 5 lessons I learned through Ninjutsu and Martial Arts and connect them to principles of truth found in the scriptures. These 5 lessons and many others became the foundation of my Spiritualjutsu!

I invite each reader to find Jesus Christ in your own personal experiences. Sometimes life is just so busy and noisy that we may miss him standing there, eagerly waiting for us to call out to him. As you read this, ask yourself, where has Christ been in my experiences? Where is Christ right now?

The 5 Lessons:

Lesson 1:   Endurance, perseverance and stealth (Luke 19:1-6)

Lesson 2:   I don't drink coffee (1 Nephi 8:26-28)

Lesson 3:   500 push-ups (Ephesians 3:20 and Mosiah 27:25)

Lesson 4:   Never the underdog (The true lesson of David and Goliath)

Lesson 5:   I will go and do… well, maybe? (1 Nephi 3:7)

Lesson 1: Endurance, Perseverance and Stealth (Luke 19:1-6)

The Jutsu

I will never forget the day: October 18, 1992. That was my first Ninjutsu class and I remember how excited I was to start. I had already been doing Karate for nearly five years at this point and received a special invitation from the head instructor to join a class of only eight students.

The Sensei walked in and demanded our attention, so we all lined up. I was loving it already — weapons and black suits with the famous ninja mask. I remember thinking how much of an advantage I would have over everyone else because I had almost five years of Karate experience and already had my black belt.

As we lined up, the Sensei started to explain in detail what we were going to learn and do over the next six months. Then we were assigned partners. These partners were a very important part of the training program. We were expected to learn and practice our techniques as well as perform all our exercises with our partner. Many of these exercises, I soon found out, involved lifting my partner and carrying them around, sometimes for the entire class.

So, there I was, awaiting my assigned partner when the Sensei called upon a boy from the back of the Dojo who had arrived late and was waiting for his invitation to join the class. I remember thinking to myself, "How old is this kid and how much does he weigh?" and "why is he so much bigger than everyone else? Is this class not organized by age group?"

My excitement turned to fear as this boy was assigned as my partner. As he ran and stood in front of me, I could no longer see anything else because he was so big. The remainder of that class was dedicated to learning the exercises we would do each class. When I got home, my mom asked how the class went. Her question was asked with much excitement as she remembered the motivated and enthusiastic young man who left earlier that evening eager to learn Ninjutsu.

"I don't think I want to go back" I said.

"Why not?" my mother replied.

"Well," I answered, "it's a long bus ride and it's probably too expensive anyways."

"I already paid for the program, so don't worry about it." my mom said. My mind went blank and I no longer could think of an excuse, so I took a deep breath and told myself it was only going to be six months.

Now let's fast forward three months from that first class. I was struggling. I could barely pick up my partner.

As I watched the other kids run around the Dojo with ease my heart sank.

On January 23, 1993 I showed up to class and my partner was not there. The Sensei pulled me aside and told me that my partner was sick, and I would be placed with another partner group for that class.

I will never forget the feeling of superhuman strength that surged through my entire body as I picked up my temporary partner. During my very first attempt to throw him on my shoulders, he went flying over my head and landed on his regular partner who was standing three feet behind us.

The class stopped. All eyes were on me. The superhuman feeling faded as the Sensei came running towards me. For a brief moment I thought I was in trouble. The boy that I threw was perfectly okay, besides the extreme fear on his face which made me realize that's how I must look when I was with my regular partner.

"Michael," said the Sensei "be careful with these guys today, they are not the same size as your normal partner."

I wish I could say that I was intuitive enough back then to really capture the powerful lessons I was learning in my first three months in Ninjutsu. The Sensei pulled me aside after that class and mentioned how proud he was of me that I stuck with it. I never forgot his words, they still ring in my ears: "Eliminate the human flaw of ego and adapt to the spiritual power of endurance and perseverance and you'll become something more."

The Spiritual

It's funny how some things stick with you despite not really understanding how significant and meaningful the lessons are at the time. Ralph Waldo Emerson said it best: "The years teach much which the days never knew."

To better understand the lesson of endurance and perseverance let's look at one of my favorite stories in the New Testament, found in Luke 19 verses 1-6.

1 And Jesus entered and passed through Jericho.

2 And, behold, there was a man named Zacchæus, which was the chief among the publicans, and he was rich.

3 And he sought to see Jesus who he was; and could not for the press, because he was little of stature.

4 And he ran before and climbed up into a sycamore tree to see him: for he was to pass that way.

5 And when Jesus came to the place, he looked up, and saw him, and said unto him, Zacchæus, make haste, and come down; for today I must abide at thy house.

6 And he made haste, and came down, and received him joyfully.

I love how verse two explains that Zacchaeus is chief among the publicans, making sure we know that he has worked his way up and received some type of promotion. This is important to understand about his personality, status and the type of worker he was.

I also enjoy that verse two clearly identifies that he was rich. This makes me think of the man who came to Jesus Christ and asked what he could do to have eternal life (Matt 19:16). After the Savior explained some important things that must be done, he invited the man to go and sell all he had and give to the poor (Matt 19:21). The rich man upon hearing this walked away sorrowful (Matt 19:22) not because of what he had done but because of what he was unwilling to do.

Jesus then taught us how rare it would be for a rich man to enter the kingdom of Heaven (Matt 19:23). So, when I read about Zacchaeus being rich, I already feel that the odds are not in his favour.

We learn something about Zacchaeus in verse three that sets him apart from the rich man in Matthew 19. The rich man wanted something from Jesus whereas Zacchaeus wanted to feel something from Jesus. The Rich man declared that he has kept the commandments since his youth which shows his obedience but when asked to give up all he has (sacrifice) he could not do it.

Zacchaeus demonstrates the power and blessings that come when we combine both obedience and sacrifice. Jesus Christ gave the invitation to see who He is when He said, "Learn of me, and listen to my words; walk in the meekness of my spirit, and you shall have peace in me" (D&C 19:23).

Zacchaeus had a desire to "see Jesus who he was." yet he could not "for the press, because he was little of stature" (Luke 19:3). What does this really mean? The press doesn't mean reporters but rather too many people. Little of stature means he's just short.

Now this is where things become pretty interesting for me, remembering back on my Ninjutsu class where I first saw my new partner.   He was like the press — large in stature. And there I was of little stature. No matter how little I felt during that first class, I hung in there, I didn't go home when I easily could have, and neither did Zacchaeus.

Now verse four is loaded with a lot of powerful principles of truth. Doing a quick glance, one might easily say he simply ran and climbed a tree. I see his effort as so much more. I feel a deep connection to Zacchaeus when I think about how far "he ran before" (Luke 19:4).

We are not told how far he ran. But we do know it was not easy due to his little stature. I can just picture his little legs working so hard to get him to a place where he "climbed up into a sycamore tree to see him: for he was to pass that way" (Luke 19:4).

The day my partner was sick and I joined the other group and picked up that kid and threw him behind me, I remember another boy telling me how light the boy must have been. Maybe he was much lighter, maybe Zacchaeus only had to run a few hundred yards, but that is not the point, is it? Because I decided to stay and endure those difficult exercises and keep going when my ego and body were shouting at me to just quit and go home, I experienced the joy of my endurance and perseverance.

The same was true for Zacchaeus, he did not go home to his fancy job and many possessions but instead, he chose to run towards Christ rather than escaping away to his familiar comforts.

I love the resourcefulness of Zacchaeus who teaches us how he learned from his previous experience of dealing with the press. This time he will climb the sycamore tree to guarantee a better view. Think about that for a moment.

Zacchaeus was not planning to speak with the Savior. His efforts to run and climb up the tree were just to see him and feel of his spirit.

Sycamore trees around Jericho are considered by many to be Ficus sycamore that can get to be 130 feet tall and as wide as seven feet in diameter. It's my personal opinion that there should be a special scouting badge for anyone who can successfully climb a sycamore tree. Can you picture this small man trying to get into this tree? What would that have looked like?

It's also important to note the transition from verse four where Zacchaeus ran and climbed to verse five when Jesus is now passing by. Let's slow down these verses and think about this question, how long did Zacchaeus wait in that sycamore tree?

It took training three days a week for three months with my partner to show me signs that my hard work of endurance and perseverance was not in vain. We know that during the Saviour's travels through Jericho he was among large crowds. This must have slowed his pace down so that it took him longer to get to places. I don't know how long Zacchaeus was waiting in that tree before he realized that his efforts were not in vain. But I do know that he got everything he earned.

I know that enduring and persevering can be extremely difficult. Listen to the invitation the Savior gave to Zacchaeus as a reward of his endurance and perseverance: "Zacchaeus, make haste, and come down; for today I must abide at thy house" (Luke 19:5).

What stands out to you in this invitation? I am humbled to hear the Savior call him by name, not "Hey you!" but rather he calls him by name. The Savior said, "I am the good shepherd, and know my sheep" (John 10:14).

My humility increases when I read the words, "I must abide at thy house." These words solidify the true power of endurance and perseverance. The Savior recognized the great efforts made by Zacchaeus just as he recognizes our great efforts.

When we are faced with challenges and trials that are much bigger than our little stature can handle, it is my hope that we will not shrink and run away. Let's remember Zacchaeus's endurance and perseverance. Let it fuel our desire to run ahead, climb high and wait as long as necessary, so we can hear the Savior tell us to hurry up and get down so we can be united with him. Let's also remember that the Savior knows us by name and will always come unto us as we try to do whatever we can. It is my hope that we will also "receive him joyfully" (Luke 19:6).

What does receive him joyfully really mean? In my personal experience I received him without any second guessing, with no hesitating and wondering if I'm actually good enough and does he really want to spend time with me. I testify that he not only wants to spend time with you but that he really loves spending time with you.

NOTES

Spiritualjutsu

Lesson 2: I don't drink coffee (1 Nephi 8:26-28)

The Jutsu

The year was 2008 and I was invited to present the concepts of the martial arts system I created to the Grandmaster and his council in Japan.

I prepared and trained for this specific event for over ten years. Thousands of hours poured into developing new movement systems, striking patterns, specially designed fitness routines and weapon-based combat strategies. These I built on a foundation of my personal philosophy of what a combat system should really mean to those that study it.

The night before I was leaving, I wanted to get a few hours of practice in to help calm my nerves. I went outside in my backyard with my recently sharpened Katana sword and was about ten minutes into my routine when I tripped and cut my leg just to the right side of my knee. I was hopeful when I first looked at it. It didn't look too bad, I thought. Then I realized it was a clean cut and it became apparent that I needed to go to the hospital.

Six stitches and two staples later I was good as new and ready to go to Japan! As you can imagine, my confidence was really rattled. I still wonder to this day if the popular mobile app game called Clumsy Ninja is based on me?

I spent the first day in Japan with six individuals who watched closely as I demonstrated my striking patterns and movement systems. On several occasions, they stopped me and asked questions. I responded and re-demonstrated my techniques for them. This became so physically exhausting that after eleven hours of demonstrating techniques I had the world's worst foot cramp. The cramp was so intense I started to walk with a limp. Several of the council members eying my limp asked, "What new movement pattern are you demonstrating now?"

The second day did not get much better. I demonstrated my weapons combat strategies by sparring with some of the most skilled sword and stick fighters on the planet. My knee had become roughly the size of a softball and felt bigger than a basketball.

Day three was the hand-to-hand combat challenge. I found myself attempting to make my first challenger submit to a triangle choke. For those who don't know, a triangle choke is when your legs are wrapped around your opponent's neck forming what looks like a triangle.

My opponent was not submitting because my legs were not tight enough against his neck. I was trying to not overdo it with my stitched and stapled up knee but once I felt my opponent starting to muster up strength to force a release, I committed to going all in no matter what would happen to my knee.

I tightened up my legs and within about ten seconds I felt a pop, pop, pop, and pop! There went four of my stitches. On the plus side, my opponent submitted to defeat by tapping out.

After the match, I made my way to the medical area where they stitched my knee back up. My next match was twenty minutes later. Thankfully, it went well. I was able to quickly use my famous dream catcher (top secret Ninja technique) to put opponent number two to sleep. It was my third opponent that really gave me trouble. This opponent was fast and seemed much stronger than me. As we fought, I could tell he wasn't going to submit. All I could think about was my injured knee.

I was able to forget about my knee for a brief moment when my opponent knocked me out for two minutes. It was a bittersweet defeat. I was not happy at losing but at least I could now go rest and get ready to meet the Grandmaster tomorrow, my final day of presenting my combat system.

Meeting the Grandmaster was one of the most inspiring experiences I have ever had. He was funny, humble and intelligent. At one point, he went into detail about the ancient ceremony that was scheduled for the following evening. At the ceremony, all the council and those who were senior instructors would gather to solidify my combat system as part of the family of Patyon Ninjutsu. The ceremony was a special dinner with cultural presentations and a reading from the scrolls of the Masters.

He spoke passionately about this ancient ceremony that occurs every ten years, the first one of its kind taking place nearly 240 years ago. He asked me if I believed in God. I found this question interesting and when I answered yes, he replied: "Tell me about him." He listened intently as I shared my testimony of Heavenly Father and when I got emotional, he reached out and touched my hand without saying a word. I felt his respect and reverence for what I had shared. I testified that the best ways I came to know Christ was when I spent more of my time practicing what he taught. My love for him has grown when I take my relationship with him out of the pages of scripture and into my feet.

The next day was the Ancient Ceremony where I witnessed marvelous displays of the art of Patyon Ninjutsu, from its inception to some of the most modern and unconventional practices. The climax of this event was the ceremonial feast of warriors. This is where things became extremely intense.

Part of this feast requires that each participant drink a small portion of aged alcohol that represents the fruit of the Bushido tree. Before each participant drinks, the Grandmaster blesses it, and everyone holds up the hilt of an old Wakizashi sword which happens to be filled with alcohol. Panicked, I looked and saw the substance in my hilt. I motioned for the ceremonial server to come over.

Once he was by my side, I explained that I was not able to participate as I did not drink alcohol. He sprung back in shock and motioned that I drink it without question. This prompted the gentleman beside me to lean over and whisper, "this is not really your traditional alcohol" and another person quickly chimed in with, "That's not even half a cup! I'm sure you won't get drunk from a few tablespoons!"

At this point, everyone was staring at me and it felt like my heart was going to burst out of my chest. I apologized and told them firmly, "I can't drink this." I heard a person say that I was being disrespectful to an ancient custom and another say I was being selfish. It felt like my body must have been shaking but this time I did not say sorry, I would no longer apologize for knowing what I knew. I picked up the hilt that contained the alcohol and placed it back on the server's tray and sat down.

There was no doubt that I was the most disliked person in the room. I could physically feel people's eyes rolling at me. The Grandmaster walked over and whispered something into the server's ear and the server left the room. It felt like the server was gone for eternity, but it was only a few minutes.

The server returned, and the Grandmaster gestured

for him to bring me the hilt. I looked into the hilt and asked the server what was in it? He replied, coffee! You must be kidding me! My heart sank for a moment but then I started laughing. I walked over to the Grandmaster and took his hand and explained why I did not drink alcohol, tea or coffee.

He, along with the eighteen other people at this feast listened to me explain the word of wisdom and eventually a new hilt was brought out. We completed the feast with everyone else drinking aged alcohol and myself drinking milk.

Afterwards, I was happy to hear a few people tell me that they admired my faith. Most did not speak to me after that, making the rest of the experience extremely lonely. President Thomas S. Monson taught:

"As we go about living from day to day, it is almost inevitable that our faith will be challenged. We may at times find ourselves surrounded by others and yet standing in the minority or even standing alone concerning what is acceptable and what is not. Do we have the moral courage to stand firm for our beliefs, even if by so doing we must stand alone?" (Dare to Stand Alone, October 2011 General Conference)

The Spiritual

When I read 1 Nephi 8:26-28 I am always amazed by this powerful dream and its meaningful symbolism. In verse 26 is the description of the great and spacious building. We read how, "it stood as it were in the air, high above the earth."

It's a scary thought for me to imagine the elevated pride that exists in the world. Also, the fact that this great and spacious building is not even touching soil. My thoughts are drawn to the parable of the sower, also known as the parable of the soil (Matt 13:3-8). The basic summary of this parable is found in the condition of the soil to which seed is placed in hopes of producing fruit.

This great and spacious building being elevated high above the ground reminds me how far these people have removed themselves from being able to cast seeds anywhere.

I can picture in my mind the great and spacious building high above the ground, where people stand and fill the building with no thought, no desire and no effort at all to at least try to sow seeds. I think about the seeds that fell by the wayside and how poor the soil conditions were but at least there was an effort to plant even if the wayside was not an ideal location.

Well, if there must be a great and spacious building, who manages it? There's no doubt in my mind that Satan is the superintendent of this great and spacious building. Perhaps one of the reasons it is placed so high above the earth is to ensure no one ever leaves. I think about King Noah who was about to release Abinadi but changed his mind as the priests worked the king up to anger and pride. The king's "priests lifted up their voices against him, and began to accuse him, saying: he has reviled the king. Therefore, the king was stirred up in anger against him, and he delivered him up that he might be slain" (Mosiah 17:11-12).

What a powerful example of what happens when the fears of looking different and not being admired by others elevate our pride high above the earth.

This is not Satan's first high school dance. His reign as superintendent of the great and spacious building began in the pre-mortal world — even the War in Heaven. Sometimes we refer to the great war in past tense as something that happened, rather than referring to this war as still happening. Satan has never stopped fighting the defenders of Jesus Christ. Knowing that this war still rages on should increase our urgency to be as well trained and prepared as any soldier should be.

No wonder 1 Nephi 8:28 explains, "and after they had tasted of the fruit, they were ashamed, because of those that were scoffing at them; and they fell away". Now, when that hilt was placed in front of me, I did not feel ashamed, but I definitely felt, awkward, embarrassed and uncomfortable. I don't know how far of a leap it is from feeling awkward, embarrassed and uncomfortable to feeling ashamed. Fortunately for me, somewhere during that experience I remembered how delicious the fruit of the tree tasted.

I always enjoy comparing the seed that Alma talked about in Alma chapter 32. When "planted in your heart" (Alma 32:28) eventually the seed we plant and nourish produces delicious fruit like that of the fruit of the Tree of Life in Lehi's dream. It's amazing to ponder how that tiny seed has the potential to grow into the mighty Tree of Life. Lehi invited his family members to partake of the fruit of that tree, so they would eventually plant the seed in their hearts and produce their own tree of life (Alma 32:41).

Hours before I was to leave Japan and return home, I was approached by a person who was present at the feast of warriors. This person had made the comment, "it's only a small amount of alcohol, just drink and get it over with."

As this person stared at me, they became emotional and so did I. I told them not to worry about what had happened and that I cherished the experience. This person became even more emotional and finally pulled me into a hug and whispered in my ear, "I am a member of the

Church of Jesus Christ of Latter-Day Saints and have struggled for years to go to church consistently. Your courage and faith reminded me of what it means to be true to yourself. Please forgive me for not standing with you."

I don't know what happened to this wonderful member of the church. What I do know is that whenever we dare to stand alone we invite the powers of Heaven to stand with us and like my wife's favorite scripture teaches us, "Fear not: for they that be with us are more than they that be with them" (2 Kings 6:16).

Notes

Lesson 3: 500 Push-ups (Nephi and the Boat, Mosiah 24:11-14 and Mosiah 27:25)

The Jutsu

While testing in Japan I only had one more challenge to go. I was nine hours into my fifth Degree Black Belt test and had already completed the first three challenges. At this point, I was beginning to struggle immensely. I found myself on an obstacle course, fifty feet in the air trying to convince myself that I was so close to finishing and that I really did not need to start crying.

I am often asked if I enjoy the TV show American Ninja Warrior. In the show, great athletes compete in a series of challenging obstacle courses that test strength, balance, stamina and strategy. I absolutely love the show!

Well, this obstacle challenge I was completing was much different than what you would see on any American Ninja Warrior show for a few reasons.

First of all, there are no masked Ninjas chasing you, attacking you and trying to stop you from reaching the finish line in any episode of American Ninja Warrior. When you add about thirty-five Ninjas spread out through a twelve-kilometer course, you realized that the American Ninja Warrior courses are walks through the park.

As I sat in a safe place to rest, I mustered enough courage to move away from my comfort zone to retrieve the last of ten tokens. Each token is awarded to participants during the course once you reached special markers. I had nine tokens and was only twenty yards from obtaining my tenth and final token. My legs felt like rubber and I could barely move. My muscles started seizing up four hours earlier when I had disarmed four Ninjas in exchange for my seventh token.

I made my way to the ground and slowly tried figuring out what I would say to the Grandmaster, who held in his hand the final token. Rumor had it that the final challenge for the tenth token was not a physical test but rather a mental one, in the form of a question or puzzle. For me this was good news, considering the astonishing physical fatigue I was feeling.

I started towards the Grandmaster, who sat on a chair, legs crossed looking like he was filled with the utmost ancient wisdom and knowledge. As I approached, he walked to me and handed me a towel and pointed to my neck. I realized that my neck was bleeding from one of the blows I received during this nine-hour torture fest. After wiping my neck, I tried handing the towel back, but he invited me to clean the rest of my wounds.

After I cleaned myself off, he motioned for me to stand and follow him. We walked for a few minutes, me walking slowly behind him until we reached the finish point. For a brief moment, all I could picture was this Grandmaster turning around and lunging forward to finish the job this obstacle course started.

He turned to face me with no signs of a looming attack but rather pulled from his pocket a token, *the* token, the final token needed to pass. I stared at this token, thinking back on the past several years of my life, the past ten hours of this crazy test and all the training and preparation that went in to receiving this last token that rested a few feet from my grasp.

"Do you want this token?" the Grandmaster asked.

"Yes, Grandmaster, I do" was my reply.

"What have you done to earn it?"

"I trained and dedicated my life to becoming prepared enough to be here right now. I defeated each challenge placed before me. I taught others to be strong and to know the way of the Ninja and will continue to teach others how to reach their personal best."

The Grandmaster smiled at me and told me that I had performed well and all that remained was a demonstration of my potential. A demonstration of my potential? How do I demonstrate my potential?

There must be a translation problem, perhaps he chose the wrong word.

He then said, while still smiling, "Drop down and do five hundred push-ups!"

I looked at him and even though I was more physically exhausted than I had ever been before, smiled and said, "I hope you're not going anywhere; this is going to take a while!"

He laughed and politely added, "Without stopping or resting please." As I was already in push-up position, with my face towards the ground, I knew he would not be able to see my tears. I lost all hope in knowing that there was no way I would be able to come close to doing five hundred push-ups in a row with no stopping or resting. I couldn't even do one hundred push-ups in a row on my best day!

My body was shaking, my hands bleeding, and I could not stop sobbing, having come so far to fail now. As I started to do the push-ups, I felt a small portion of despair leave me, replaced by a fresh wave of determination. I kept telling myself "Just keep swimming, just keep swimming."

I wasn't even counting. I kept my head down and just kept doing push-ups. At a certain point reality really set in and I knew I wasn't going to be able to do any more push-ups. I took one big gasp of air and bit my lip as I slowly pushed up from my final, but clearly not my five hundredth push-up.

Then, my arms gave out and I crashed to the ground in what felt like an embarrassing feat of exhaustion, failure and humiliation. I would like to save face here and say that I was proud for trying my hardest and giving it my all, but in reality, I was actually wondering if I would ever be able to pick myself up from the ground. I felt like such a failure, I was not only exhausted, I was devastated.

I laid on the ground for a long time before I mustered the courage to look up towards the Grandmaster. When I did, I was surprised to see the Grandmaster grinning at me. His eyes seemed to reflect a sense of pride and in my mind, I could just picture him saying, "Another one bites the dust — literally."

I looked away briefly to clear that thought out of my head, then looked back at the Grandmaster and the translator who now joined him, to see the translator wink at me. The wink is a funny thing. But this wink carried with it the boost that I needed to get to my feet and walk up to the Grandmaster to accept my failure —and kiss my tenth token goodbye.

As I walked towards the Grandmaster, I could see that grin that was still plastered on his face. He reached for me and hugged me close while the translator said, calling me by name, "Great job Michael!" I pulled back a little and asked in a confused tone, "Did I do the 500 push-ups? I wasn't counting." The translator smiled at me and said, "not even close."

I felt like I was about to drop like a stone to the ground again due to the heaviness of my heart, but I stayed calm and accepted my defeat. Then something happened that really had me confused. The Grandmaster took my hand and placed in the center of my palm the tenth and final token. I stared at it and of course when I looked up at the Grandmaster, he still had that grin which at this point I assumed was tattooed on his face.

I did not question what was happening, instead I quickly bowed and walked away thinking to myself, *this guy clearly can't count.* With my ten tokens in hand I was ready to present them to the Head Grandmaster at the ceremony where I would receive my Fifth Degree Black Belt.

That whole evening and next morning I felt terrible. I knew I hadn't completed the challenge. I had not done five hundred push-ups. It did not matter how hard I tried or how many I actually did; I hadn't passed the test. I could not stand feeling the guilt, so I made up my mind that I was going to give the tenth token back.

Later that afternoon I entered the dining hall and anxiously sought out the Grandmaster. Once I saw him, I quickly grabbed a translator and walked over to him. I reverently called his name and when he turned around, I bowed, thrust out my hand and said, "I did not do the five hundred push-ups you asked me to do and I do not deserve this final token."

Once I heard the translator start speaking, I felt a huge burden lifted off my shoulders. I knew I was doing the right thing. The Grandmaster spoke, telling me to stand up straight. He took a few steps until he was right in front of me and said in broken, yet understandable English, "If I only asked you to do one hundred push-ups, you would not have done two hundred and eleven."

As I looked at his face and that unforgettable grin, he pulled me in close and with his right arm around my waist lifted up his left hand as high as he could and said, "aim high, not low". He walked away, and I was left there staring at the token.

The Spiritual Part 1:

"Now unto him that is able to do exceedingly abundantly above all that we ask or think, according to the power that worketh in us." (Ephesians 3:20)

There is no denying the reality that God does in fact expect much from us, but that's because he is actively making something of us each and every day, if we let him.

This amazing Grandmaster who asked me to do five hundred push-ups did not care if I could do all of them, he cared about what I would become by trying to do all of them. All these push-ups he wanted me to do were the vehicle to get me there.

Our Heavenly Father knows that our mortal experiences are filled with what I now call five hundred push-up moments. Moments where we feel life is too hard and the challenge or trial is too big. It is in these moments that Heavenly Father never asks us to do less for ourselves but rather stay focused on having us do *all* that we possibly can. Heavenly Father, like the Grandmaster, is making us into something he knows will prepare us for much more than the current challenge or trial at hand.

In his message entitled *Lessons from Liberty Jail*, Elder Jeffery R. Holland reminds us that, "man's extremity is God's opportunity."

Just what is God's opportunity then? In my case, it was when I realized that I could do more than I ever thought I could and was extended grace to make up the difference when I couldn't do all the push-ups. During that process, I connected with a power that worked inside me and kept me going when everything else in my body screamed at me to stop.

I was changed that day. My heart and mind were transformed into something more than what they were before. This never would have happened if I was only asked to do one hundred push-ups. We will never become more than what we are now if we are only asked to do what we know we can already do, in other words one hundred push-ups. Especially when Heavenly Father knows we can do more. He knows we have two hundred and eleven push-ups inside ourselves, but we will not get there if we are only trying for a hundred.

That's why Heavenly Father asks us to do more. Because he is making something more out of each of us.

I often wonder who Nephi would have become if early one morning he woke up and found a boat sitting in the water already built and ready to use. How much learning and personal development would have been lost if the Lord did not ask Nephi to build that boat under the condition's he had built it?

Nephi was asked to do five hundred push-ups many times throughout his life and as a result, he learned to trust the Lord (211 push-ups) and rely on his grace to make up the remaining 289.

The Spiritual Part 2:

Speaking about that "power that worketh in us" (Ephesians 3:20), I have felt further comfort in moments of challenge from the redeemed Alma the Younger, who, after receiving strength to his limbs declared how through "being redeemed of God" we become "his sons and daughters" (Mosiah 27:25).

That word redeemed is something of great worth to my experience with those five hundred push-ups. After all the push-ups I was able to do, I was still short of the full amount that was asked of me.

The reality is, we will be asked to do great things and endure many things, and often times we will fall short but that's where the grace of Jesus Christ comes to our rescue.

When we take the time to recognize the potential for growth that resides within every challenge we face, we will always see Jesus Christ. Alma and his people felt his redeeming power when Amulon was willing to put to death anyone who was caught praying (Mosiah 24:11).

It is also clear in Mosiah 24:12-14 that Alma recognized the potential for growth from this experience as he invited the people to "pour out their hearts to him" and by doing this the Lord took all the push-ups they could do and made the remaining push-ups easier when he declared that "even you cannot feel them upon your backs."

It is evident that God expects much from us because he is making something of us. He doesn't just love us because he has to, he loves us because we're his (Mosiah 5:7, 27:25).

The Spiritual Part 3:

As the Jaredites travelled to the promised land, they found themselves on the water for three hundred and forty-four days. During this time on the sea, they experienced some very intense and powerful storms.

"And it came to pass that they were many times buried in the depths of the sea, because of the mountain waves which broke upon them, and also the great and terrible tempests which were caused by the fierceness of the wind." (Ether 6:6)

I often replace the words "sea" with life (mortality) and "winds and waves" with trials, struggles and difficulties. The verse takes on a more personal meaning as I do that. Because we all experience our own personal storms and at times feel as if we are buried in the depths of challenge and struggle, we can really feel for these faithful, yet endangered, Jaredites.

It becomes even more interesting when we jump back to Ether 6:5 which says:

"And it came to pass that the Lord God caused that there should be a <u>furious wind</u> blow upon the face of the waters, <u>towards</u> the promised land; and thus they were tossed upon the waves of the sea before the wind."

Sometimes, not all the time, but in the important times of our lives, it's the Lord who causes the challenges, trials, struggles and difficulties to come into our lives. In verse 5 we learn that the Lord caused the furious wind to blow upon the waters and when we paraphrase and personalize the words found in verse 5, they read like this:

"And it just so happened that the Lord God provided difficult challenges and trials to come into their lives as he worked to make something of them; and so, they continually faced difficult challenges in life while growing into something better."

The Lord is taking us to places that are significant to our personal growth and development. He is more concerned with our personal growth than he is our desire to enjoy the comfort of a calm, windless, and waveless sea. How do you feel knowing God is more concerned with your growth than he is your comfort?

When the Lord asks you to do five hundred push-ups, remember, he is inviting you to see beyond what you and others may see. He is causing you to move towards bigger and better things. He is making something of you.

NOTES

Lesson 4: Never the Underdog (The true lesson of David and Goliath)

The Jutsu

I remember the day I decided that I wanted to serve a full-time mission for the Church of Jesus Christ of Latter-Day Saints. I had other plans several years in the works before being baptized when I was seventeen years old. These plans changed after I found the gospel.

Following my baptism, I found myself working with the missionaries a few days each week. I would meet them at the church, and we would head out to appointments with those who wanted to learn more about the gospel, members of the church, members who were no longer attending regularly and, of course, to knock on doors to find new people to teach. For the first several weeks of going out with the missionaries I loved the work we were doing.

I remember one day perfectly. It was April 8th, 1998 around 7:30 pm. The missionaries and I decided to knock on some doors after an appointment fell through. We knocked on the door of an elderly man who was about seventy years old. He seemed excited to speak with us. He invited us inside which, for any missionary, is one of the most satisfying feelings in the world.

This feeling was short lived. As we walked into the living room there were two dozen other people ranging in ages from fourteen to eighty. They were all holding bibles in their hands. It became clear in my mind that this was some sort of bible study group. Without any chance to introduce ourselves, the man who welcomed us into his home began questioning some of the foundational doctrines of the Church of Jesus Christ of Latter-Day Saints.

The missionaries were clearly thrown off but did well in answering the questions. The questions turned into statements that were spoken in such anger and animosity that there was no longer any chance to speak and share our thoughts and responses. Near the end, one of the other people stood up and declared, "How can you think for one second that a fourteen-year-old boy like Joseph Smith, with no education and influence could see God and be trusted to share such a powerful message like the one he said he had?"

"Go back to Utah and take your Mormon bible with you," another person immediately chimed in. The missionaries were polite and thanked them for their time and started heading to the door. This entire time I just stood there listening to these people insult, mock and sneer at the truths I had grown not only to love but knew were true. I wanted to say something, but what could I say? I did not know the bible well enough to engage in a conversation with these folks, and as a new member of the church, I was still learning about my new faith.

As I started to walk away, I felt a strong impression come over me that elevated my confidence and courage to a level that caused me to turn and invite one of the people from the group to turn to Matthew 5:8 and read it so everyone could hear. They read out loud, "Blessed are the pure in heart: for they shall see God."

At the conclusion of that verse being read I asked this question: "What is the qualification to see God?"

The man who had invited us into the home spoke first and declared, "A pure heart."

"That's right." I said. I then declared that it does not say how much experience one must have, how much education they need or how old they have to be in order to see God.

Someone shouted from the group, "It means that they must have lived a good life in order to see God in the next." To which I said: "Thanks for sharing, but it doesn't say you must be dead first, it simply speaks to the condition of one's heart. Joseph Smith had a sincere heart and real intent. Because of that, not only did he see what he said he saw, but he helps magnify the truth of the Bible and prove that God does fulfill his promises."

After I was done speaking there was absolute silence. I said nothing, the missionaries said nothing, and we felt the need to leave at that moment of significant silence.

That night I got home and dropped to my knees in prayer. I thanked Heavenly Father for the gift of the Holy Ghost. I then asked him if I should serve a full-time mission. He answered, "Yes Michael, you should serve a mission and teach others what I taught you tonight."

Jutsu Part 2: The Grandmasters Championship Tournament

Once I decided I wanted to serve a mission I needed to save some money and get serious about my game plan. There was a special tournament I could compete in to earn some cash. There were five areas of competition:

1) **Combat** (Full contact hand to hand fighting)
2) **Weapons Combat** (You choose your weapon and you fight others with the same or different weapons)
3) **Kata** (Grouped techniques performed in sequence)
4) **Weapons Kata** (Grouped techniques performed in sequence with your chosen weapon)
5) **Obstacle Course** (a 30-minute course with several challenges testing strength, endurance and resourcefulness)

This tournament would determine the winners based on points you earned from finishing in the top five of each event. The points were awarded as follows:

1ST PLACE-   **500 POINTS**

2nd PLACE-   **300 POINTS**

3rd PLACE-   **200 POINTS**

4th PLACE-   **100 POINTS**

5th PLACE-   **50 POINTS**

I competed fairly well in this tournament in past years. One year I even finished 7th place. If you finished in the overall top three, you would win money and prizes. At the time, one of the sponsors was Kawasaki and you could get a dirt bike along with prize money.

Preparation for this three-day tournament would be intense, so I decided not to compete because I needed to work an extra job to eventually help pay for my mission. Shortly after I made the decision not to compete, I picked up another job.

One day while I was doing my normal Tuesday night Ninjutsu routine, I had a strong impression come to me that I should compete in the Grandmaster Championships. I figured it was because I loved the competition and was in the middle of doing Ninjutsu, so I shrugged it off and finished my workout.

That impression did not leave me, and it became stronger, so I took it to the Lord in prayer and asked if I should compete. I did not feel any answer, so I did not do anything. Several days after, the feeling to compete increased. When I shared these feelings with my friend Ed, he shared that I was not experiencing a stupor of thought, and that it was important I continued to pray about it since the feeling remained strong and consistent.

I walked away from that conversation and looked up the word stupor. Stupor is feeling dazed, confused and not really being able to figure something out. My friend Ed got his insight from Doctrine and Covenants section 9:8-9:

8 But, behold, I say unto you, that you must study it out in your mind; then you must ask me if it be right, and if it is right I will cause that your bosom shall burn within you; therefore, you shall feel that it is right.

9 But if it be not right you shall have no such feelings, but you shall have a stupor of thought that shall cause you to forget the thing which is wrong; therefore, you cannot write that which is sacred save it be given you from me.

I spent the next several days praying if I should dedicate the time to be in this tournament. The council found in Doctrine and Covenants 9:8 became alive as I felt a burning in my heart. I also felt a very specific message that day which told me if I practiced hard and had faith, I would win the tournament and would be able to go on my mission.

When I got off my knees the natural man set in and I remember thinking: *How am I going to beat the other guys who are far better than me? I can't win this tournament!*

In perceiving my thoughts, I felt another specific message come into my heart saying, "Do what I ask, and you will be blessed."

Do What I Ask

In the past, I spent nearly four days a week in the dojo and gym preparing for this tournament. As I organized my schedule, I realized that in order to keep working my part-time jobs and train effectively for this tournament, I would need to cut back on my seminary make-up work.

When I was baptized at seventeen, I decided I wanted to try and get all four years of seminary done so I could graduate. To do this, I met with my amazing seminary teacher and created a learning plan. Up to this point I was doing really well but now my time needed to be dedicated to my jobs and this tournament.

One evening as I was gathering my training gear, I felt a peaceful feeling come over me that seized upon me in a way that I had not felt before. The spirit seemed to paralyze me from grabbing my gear and led me to my scriptures. My heart was drawn to the scriptures and I heard the spirit tell me to read, study and grow.

I would love to say that I ended up staying and having a wonderful experience, but I allowed my fear of not being ready for the tournament to set in and headed off to the gym. While I was at the gym and not for very long, I felt weak and extremely uncomfortable. The guys I was training with noticed I was off and asked if I was feeling alright.

I told the guys that I was not feeling well and needed to go home. When I returned home, I went straight to my room and opened my scriptures. I studied for a few hours and never felt so good. The next day I chose to study the scriptures instead of going to the gym and did that for the next several days.

One day I heard a knock at my door, and it ended up being a friend that I was training with who was also going to be in the tournament. He was wondering where I had been, and I told him I was taking some time off to do some other preparations. "What preparations?" he asked.

I felt bad that I had not shown up to train and felt that this friend deserved an explanation. "Do you remember when I joined the Church of Jesus Christ of Latter-Day Saints?"

"Yes" he replied.

"Well" I responded, "I'm entering this tournament to help pay for a two-year mission I want to go on."

"Should you not be practicing as often as you can?" He replied in confusion.

"That would make sense," I responded, "But I believe I need to study and prepare for the tournament with less physical training and more spiritual training, and if I do this I will win." I can still remember his face. He tried refraining from laughing out loud so he could respect our friendship. He finally said that it made no sense and that if I wanted to win, I should be increasing my time at the dojo, not training less.

"You're right," I said, "that is what makes logical sense, but I believe that if I do what has been asked of me that I will be blessed." As I walked my friend outside to say goodbye, he turned to me and shared a few true tournament statistics.

He said: "You know that you have never finished in the top five of this tournament and that the top guy who won the tournament five years in a row has never lost, right?" As he walked away, I remember thinking to myself, *I am training spiritually so that I can trust God's promises more than the statistics!*

The Tournament

I spent the night before the tournament alone in the hotel reflecting on the incredible journey it took to arrive at this moment. That friend of mine who was also competing was actually in the room across from me and at one point when I first arrived said, "Is Jesus still holding your hand?" I actually laughed and appreciated his sarcasm.

The next day I woke up early and knelt down for my morning prayer. I'll never forget that prayer because when I tried to speak, nothing came out of my mouth, I was just too emotional for some reason. I knelt there on the floor with tears streaming down my face. When I was finally able to speak, all I could say was, "thank you!"

I knew I was guided to that moment and I knew I was going to win that tournament!

Tournament Day 1

The first event was the weapons combat where I used my wooden sword known as a bokken. In my first match, I competed against a guy who was using a sword as well. I felt different during this match compared to the many times I had fought before. It's hard to explain how I felt. I felt a spiritual assurance come over me. It made me think of the scripture heroes that often seem to pass through situations with a steady assurance that things will work out even if they have no idea how.

I beat the first guy and every other person that day including the defending champion who for the first time in five years lost in the weapons combat. Winning earned me five hundred points. I was amazed at how my heart felt when I won, I mean I felt completely void of personal pride and boastfulness and instead was filled with gratitude. I knew why I won and where the strength came from. I felt humbled knowing that my success that day was the Lord's.

The second competition was the obstacle course. I finished third overall and earned another two hundred points. After the obstacle course, that same friend came up to me. He didn't say anything, he just stared at me with a smile. I smiled back and asked him how he was doing. He looked at me and said, "Not as well as you."

Tournament Day 2

On the morning of the second tournament day, I knelt down to say my morning prayer. Unlike the day before, today I had plenty to say. I expressed my sincere gratitude for all that happened the previous day. While I was praying, I had this feeling enter my heart that was a sincere love for the others I was competing against.

When I arrived at the tournament, I noticed the first competition was kata, which is a series of footwork and striking patterns performed in a specific order. I was ninth on the schedule. When it was my turn, I performed my routine with very little error. During the second round I added a front flip followed by a front shoulder roll and halfway through it, sprung up from the side to land on my feet. I remember thinking to myself as I landed it, "well, that's new!"

I finished second overall, just missing out on a first-place finish to the defending tournament champion. After the kata competition, the defending tournament champion approached me and stared me down. He got close enough to my face to let me know he had a tuna sandwich for lunch. Leaning in he said, "I own this tournament and I own you!" Yikes. He sure convinced me of my underdog status.

As I was preparing for the weapons kata competition, I could not find my sword anywhere. In a sudden panic, I realized I had forgotten it at the hotel. I quickly asked the tournament officials if I could go get it from the hotel. They said no and that if I was not present in ten minutes for the start of the competition I would be disqualified!

I had been taught to use many weapons in combat situations. Yet the weapons kata required participants to perform a perfect routine with their chosen weapon. Each move had to be perfect. This competition was a demonstration of power, balance and expert skill with a weapon. I had spent years working on my routine with my sword. That sword was my best chance at winning this competition.

One of the tournament officials came to remind me that I had five minutes until I had to check in. I normally enjoy punctuality. But since I had no sword, I was praying for every clock and watch to stop working immediately.

A friend of mine that I had not seen in a few years

who also uses the bokken sword as his primary weapon was sitting only a few feet from the performance stage. I hustled over to him and quickly asked if I could use his sword for the competition. He turned behind him and grabbed his escrima sticks. Escrima sticks are two pieces of bamboo, anywhere between 21 to 27 inches in length.

"This is what I'm using today, Mike," he said. "I have an extra set if you want to use them." Just as he finished pulling them out and asking me again if I wanted to use them, one of the tournament officials was heard speaking over the PA system.

"All B group competitors to stage two for weapons kata, that's all B group competitors to stage two for weapons kata for check in and rank assignment."

I grabbed my friend's extra pair of escrima sticks, said thank you and headed over to stage two. As I headed over to the stage, I realized that there was a really good chance that I would not be in the group of competitors to go first. Suddenly, I felt a huge weight disappear from my shoulders. I would have some time to practice with my escrima sticks.

I walked up to the rank assignment sheet to see when I was slotted to perform. My eyes bulged out of my face and my heart felt like it stopped all together. There was my name in slot number one. I have never, ever gone first, why now? I uttered a quick prayer inside my mind saying to Heavenly Father, "I thought I was going to win this thing?"

As I collected my thoughts, I said a prayer apologizing to Heavenly Father. I asked for forgiveness. I felt peace return to me and with it a hope that filled my body from my head to my toes. Into my mind came the words found in Doctrine and Covenants 6:36, "Look unto me in every thought; doubt not, fear not."

As I climbed onto the performance platform, I felt so good inside, I remember not thinking about my missing sword and the fact that I was about to compete with a weapon I had not used seriously in several years. I walked to the center of the platform and stood in front of the panel of five judges. I bowed my head. This is done in respect for the judges. But in that moment, I bowed a little longer for Heavenly Father.

I don't really remember anything that happened for the next few minutes. But whatever I did was met with great applause. One of the judges was even standing and clapping!

I remember thinking that something wonderful has just happened and the judges think it was my kata. But I knew it was so much more than that.

I exited the stage and was swarmed by a multitude of spectators and fellow competitors. They congratulated me on my performance. I quickly left the crowd and found a quiet place to kneel down in prayer. I thanked my Heavenly Father for blessing me with the increased capacity to do something that seemed impossible.

In that moment, I learned very clearly that what makes God so extraordinary is what he does with the ordinary.

By the time my second performance came around, I was pretty excited to compete again. I made sure to practice during the break. What I noticed was just how sloppy my foot work was. At one point, I hit myself in the back of the head with one of the sticks!

As I checked the back of my head to make sure I wasn't bleeding, I looked up and thought, *I am sure glad you're doing this with me.*

My second performance was not that exciting, and I felt the crowd had doubled in size around stage two, probably in high expectations that I would deliver another outstanding weapons kata. Well, I scored much lower this time, but my first-round performance was high enough that I walked away tied for first place with —guess who? The reigning tournament champion.

Back at the hotel I sat at the edge of my bed — tired, nervous, sore and excited to finish the tournament the next day. Knowing that the Lord got me this far, I got on my knees to thank him for everything. I felt a reassuring feeling impress upon my heart and mind that I had done my part and the Lord was pleased.

Arriving at the tournament the next morning I could see that I was two hundred points from first place, which meant I needed to finish first overall to tie the reigning tournament champion for the most points.

On the agenda for the final day of the tournament was combat competitions. Combat competitions were ten-minute continuous matches. The match only stops when a person is submitted due to strikes, is no longer capable of defending themselves, or they tap out. If the match reaches ten minutes, the match goes to the judges score card where the fighter with more points would win.

Match 1

As I looked over at my opponent, I felt confident and calm. When the judge dropped his hand signaling the start of the match, I eased my way into position for a takedown. I secured my opponents left leg and dragged him down until I was able to roll him over. I was on the bottom but still had my legs wrapped around him which is known as a full guard position.

This was a very comfortable position for me. In fact, I had developed some unorthodox techniques from this position. When my opponent tried to stand while my legs were around his waist, I dropped my right leg to the inside of his left knee and hooked my right leg around his knee to secure a knee bar. He tapped quickly, and I was victorious.

Match 2

This short match started with my opponent lunging forward with a front kick. It ended when I responded by catching them with a fading right hook to the jaw, securing my victory.

Match 3

This time, as I stood across from my opponent, I was surprised that I felt so calm. Standing across from me was the same person who eliminated me for the last two years and finished the last three tournaments in second place overall.

I could tell when he looked at me all he saw was his previous victories over me. I said a quick prayer in my heart asking for direction about what my strategy should be. I felt impressed to stare at my opponent's feet and hands. Then a wise voice whispered to me, "See those? Don't let them hit you."

As I smiled to myself and chuckled at the obvious yet vital advice, I noticed that my opponent was taken back and distracted by my smile. His distraction gave me enough time to catch him with a takedown where I ended up in full mount control on top of him (really this just means he had no use of his legs). I threw a few effective strikes from that position, but my opponent was stronger than I was, and he quickly got to his feet. Once upon my feet I felt an impression to "just keep smiling."

My smile had a dramatic impact on my opponent's ability to remain focused. Again, I found him slower than normal. I took immediate advantage and connected with a low leg round house kick followed by a hook kick from the same leg. This kick caught him square in the chin. He dropped fast and just like that it was over, securing my victory.

Match 4

From the moment the judge dropped his arm to start the fight, I was on my back. Normally I am very happy to fight from my back. But this guy was clearly much better than me on the ground. He was too good.

I was able to get up only to be taken down again and again. I was never the best fighter at these tournaments, but it was very rare for me to be taken to the ground so easily. I felt moments of panic but remembered the Lord's promises. At times it seemed that the bigger fight was not with my opponent but with myself, as I tried to remain faithful in remembering what the Lord promised and had already done for me.

As I held strong to the promises, I felt my strength increase. From my back, I was able to get into full guard position and have my legs around my opponent's waist. As he lifted up and positioned his legs to lift me off my back, I released the grip of my feet that were locked together behind his back to quickly bring my feet to the front of my body.

Once in this position and while holding on to my opponent's wrists, I placed my feet into the front part of my opponent's hips and lifted him up while still holding onto his wrists.

I twisted my hips a little and collapsed my feet at the same time. I adjusted my hands to both be on his left arm. My opponents body fell between my legs and I secured an armbar. At 9:32 seconds into the match, my opponent tapped out. If that match would have lasted another twenty-eight seconds and gone to the judges for a decision, I would have lost.

After my fourth match there was only one that remained. It was against the reigning tournament champion. He was undefeated and had not lost a hand-to-hand combat match.

This tournament was never a large-scale event. But when I jumped up unto the main platform for that final match, it seemed like there were thousands of people watching this last contest.

During my final preparations before the match started, several friends from my dojo approach me. I thought they would offer me some much-needed support and encouragement. I was surprised and saddened by their negativity.

One friend said, "you made it this far, but your luck is going to run out, you're not in that guy's league."

Another said, "you better keep praying to God that Eric (the reigning champion) doesn't embarrass you too bad."

I walked away feeling frustrated. With friends like that, who needs enemies. As I tried shaking off their mocking, I could hear the crowd cheer for the reigning champion as he made his way to the platform. The crowd almost in unison started shouting "6 in a row, 70 and 0" over and over again, getting louder and louder.

This chant was referring to him winning his sixth straight tournament and beating me to get his seventieth victory without a single loss. As we faced each other, I could not hear a word the judge was saying because of the chanting of the crowd. Did this guy bring his entire extended family to this tournament? My opponent looked at me and instead of touching gloves he withheld his respect. With a big smile on his face he repeated the crowd's chant so only I could hear: "6 in a row, 70 and 0."

We walked to our separate corners in anticipation of starting the match. I received one of the most powerful messages from Heaven in my entire life. It still gives my goosebumps, goosebumps! In that moment, I heard Heaven tell my mind and heart: "69-1."

Final Match

My opponent immediately came at me with an aggressive set of combination strikes which I defended. Next thing I knew, I was taken down and it seemed it was raining punches. As he was pouring down strikes, I managed to free my legs and roll him over unto his back. This only lasted a second as he was able to roll me over again but this time, I had my legs around his waist.

I could tell he was still very strong from this position as he continued to throw his punches. As I positioned my arms over my face in an attempt to protect myself in benefit of my future wife (you're welcome, Crystal) I noticed he was really pulling his right arm back to generate more power in those punches. As he pulled back his right arm, I quickly shifted over to the right so my right leg could go deeper around his back. I timed his punches and as he pulled his right arm back my right leg was far enough around him that my right foot hooked under his right elbow. As he went to punch, my foot stopped him, and this freed my left leg to come in towards me and up and around the back of his neck.

I was able to free his right arm at this point to get my right leg over to my left foot and secure a triangle choke. For the first time in what seemed like forever, the crowd was silenced. As I held him in this position and applied pressure in an attempt to submit him, I looked at the clock and saw that the match had not past the one-minute mark yet. This defending champion did not tap out because he was too busy being unconscious. We won the match in less than a minute! I trust you know why I say we won the match and not I won the match!

On a side note, I did win the Kawasaki dirt bike. I sold the dirt bike which added to my mission fund. I was also able to get all my seminary make up work done and graduated seminary!!

The Spiritual - The True Lesson of David and Goliath

As a kid, I loved reading about David and Goliath, and now, as an adult I love reading about David and Goliath even more. Ask anyone the question, "What is the greatest underdog story in the history of the world?" Almost every single time people will respond with the story of David and Goliath.

For years now, the story of David and Goliath has

been used to enlarge the fighting spirit to never give up and believe that the impossible can be achieved. After all, David was a simple shepherd boy, a stranger to the art of war, and yet he beat the mighty Goliath.

The words of Saul to David were like the words of my Dojo friends before my final match when they had no confidence in me to win. Saul said, "Thou art not able to go against this Philistine to fight with him: for thou art but a youth, and he a man of war from his youth." (1 Samuel 17:33)

According to Saul, David simply did not match up to the stature, skill and experience of Goliath. This is why David for centuries has been billed as the underdog. Yet David tried to help Saul understand why he wanted to fight Goliath and was not afraid. Here's what David taught Saul:

"And David said unto Saul, thy servant kept his father's sheep, and there came a lion, and a bear, and took a lamb out of the flock:

And I went out after him, and smote him, and delivered it out of his mouth: and when he arose against me, I caught him by his beard, and smote him, and slew him.

Thy servant slew both the lion and the bear: and this uncircumcised Philistine shall be as one of them, seeing he hath defied the armies of the living God.

David said moreover, The Lord that delivered me out of the paw of the lion, and out of the paw of the bear, he will deliver me out of the hand of this Philistine. And Saul said unto David, Go, and the Lord be with thee." (1 Samuel 17:34-37)

As I ponder David's words to Saul, I can clearly see that David knows something that Saul and others don't know. Reading this account makes me ask this question, did David in this moment consider himself the underdog?

The answer is in David's conversation with Goliath. Here's what Goliath said to David:

"And when the Philistine looked about, and saw David, he disdained him: for he was but a youth, and ruddy, and of a fair countenance.

And the Philistine said unto David, Am I a dog, that thou comest to me with staves? And the Philistine cursed David by his gods.

And the Philistine said to David, Come to me, and I will give thy flesh unto the fowls of the air, and to the beasts of the field." (1 Samuel 17: 42-44)

Clearly Goliath was not impressed by David. Here's what David said to Goliath:

"Then said David to the Philistine, Thou comest to me with a sword, and with a spear, and with a shield: but I come to thee in the name of the Lord of hosts, the God of the armies of Israel, whom thou hast defied.

This day will the Lord deliver thee into mine hand; and I will smite thee, and take thine head from thee; and I will give the carcases of the host of the Philistines this day unto the fowls of the air, and to the wild beasts of the earth; that all the earth may know that there is a God in Israel.

And all this assembly shall know that the Lord saveth not with sword and spear: for the battle is the Lord's, and he will give you into our hands." (1 Samuel 17:45-47)

So, ask yourself the question again, did David in this moment consider himself the underdog?

When I think back on my experience in that tournaments final match, I no longer hear the crowd cheering for the Goliath I fought that day when they yelled out, "6 in a row, 70 and 0" but rather I hear the still small voice say, "69-1."

My heart is full, knowing that when we stand in the presence of any and all opposition with the Lord, we are never the underdog. Speaking of King David, I love his description of how the Lord magnified his opportunities when he said, "Thou hast enlarged my steps under me, that my feet did not slip." (Psalms 18:36)

We might often feel like the underdog in our own stories, but we are not. The mighty and powerful Goliath was the underdog. Anyone who fights the fight alone, without the Lord is the underdog. The actual definition of underdog comes from the 19th century dog fights where the losing dog would be termed "underdog". Anyone who puts there trust in the Lord will always be the top dog.

If you feel like an underdog right now because of the size of your challenges, I invite you to remember that no problem is too big or too small for the Lord. If your trust remains centered on the Lord, all your Goliath size challenges will become the underdog of your story.

NOTES

Lesson 5: I will go and do - well, maybe? (1 Nephi 3:7)

The Jutsu

I received a phone call from a friend who was a martial arts teacher. He called to ask me if I would teach a student from his Dojo who had been struggling with not being able to get off the ground when taken there by an opponent. The student's teacher said the student was a real natural and up until recently was progressing well towards a big tournament.

I agreed to go to the Dojo and meet with this student. I arrived a few minutes early and was quickly greeted by my friend who invited me to sit and watch this particular student finish a sparring session. As I watched, I was impressed with this young woman.

She was fast — very fast. Her kicks were powerful. She had sticks of dynamite for hands because every time she landed a punch on her sparring partner the sparring partner fell down. I was very impressed and started to think that maybe her problem of being taken to the ground was simply frustration for being too dependent on her stand up fighting skills.

Then it happened. Her sparring partner, after taking a little too many dynamite punches, took the fight to the ground and started to work on a submission. This student, had been completely dominant and in control standing up, was now a completely different fighter on the ground. I could tell she wanted desperately to get up, but something was holding her back.

The student's sparring partner eventually secured a choke hold and the sparring session was over. After the student cleaned up and rested, we met.

After introductions, I remember asking heavenly Father for an increased spiritual awareness as to where to take the conversation next. So, I said, "explain to me how it feels when you're taken to the ground." She looked at me with a very frustrated and serious face. Her face was so serious that I was anticipating one of her dynamite punches to come hurling at my face.

Her serious expression turned to anger and then to sadness and then I saw it — doubt and fear covered not only her face but was clearly visible from her head to her toes. She remained silent. "Well," I said, "Whatever happened, I'm sorry it hurts so much." I got up from my chair and said I was going to get us some water.

As I walked away, she asked: "Have you ever been so afraid, that it caused you to panic, hyperventilate and feel like your entire body is paralyzed?"

I sat back down in my chair, "you bet," I said. I told her of the time I first got knocked out in a tournament. She smiled!

"I remember a few days after the tournament I was back in the Dojo sparring around like normal. My sparring partner landed a few heavy (powerful) shots. I froze and felt I was living the knockout experience all over again."

She quickly interjected, "how did you stop yourself from feeling that way?"

"Well, I don't think I've ever stopped feeling a little fear. I remember how that knock out made me feel and how it makes me feel right now."

"Great," she said, "so I'm stuck feeling this way forever."

I smiled and asked, "why don't you tell me your knockout story."

She started off slow but eventually she was fully into the conversation and telling me her story. As she shared her feelings, I could see the dynamite come back, just talking about it was a positive experience for her. Her experience was much like mine: she was defeated on the ground and put in an armbar and when she tried to get out, she fractured her arm.

"Thanks for sharing your experience with me" I told her. Over the next six weeks we worked on many things without spending any time working on her ground game. There were even a few times in sparring where she landed a few shots on me that literally took my breath away because she hit so hard.

We spent time talking about how our past defeats made us feel and how those experiences are tremendous learning tools. They help us make changes and evolve our skills by not only developing our current talents, but also developing our weaknesses. She started to look more and more confident.

The last three weeks before the tournament I taught her footwork patterns that were designed to avoid take downs. She worked on them for a few hours each day. It was amazing to see her catch on so fast.

In the last week of our training, I presented her with the game plan that I wanted her to focus on in each match of the upcoming tournament. She looked it over and was thrilled. I had built a game plan and strategy that required her never to go to the ground if she followed the plan and did things correctly. No wonder she was thrilled, the plan provided her an opportunity to avoid the hard and scary things.

The day of the tournament arrived. She had practiced and prepared each and every move sequence over and over again. She knew the game plan and was ready. Here's a quick recap of her first three matches:

Match 1- Won by TKO (technical knockout due to overwhelming amount of strikes that could not be defended)

Match 2- Won by TKO

Match 3- Won by TKO

During these matches there were some attempts to take her to the ground that made me hold my breath a few times, but she stuck to that game plan. After her 3rd match, we had a great chat about what was working. She only had one more match remaining for the championship.

"I *so* got this." she exclaimed, not with arrogance but a real confidence in her ability and in the plan. I smiled and told her to hand me the folder that had all the training notes. I took a piece of paper out of my pocket, unfolded it and placed it at the back of the section entitled game plan. She looked at me and asked what I was doing. I said I am adding the final piece to the game plan, please study it and do it exactly the way I have explained. I then got up and walked away for ten minutes.

When I came back, I found her sitting in the same place with her head in her hands. I pulled my chair up close to her and asked if she had any questions. She took a while to look up at me but when she did, she did not stop looking at me. Anyone could tell right away that she felt betrayed.

When she finally spoke, she asked a question: "Are you serious?"

"Very" I replied.

"I can't do this! This was not what the game plan was, and you can't just ask me to do something that will cost me the tournament."

"We did not come here to win you this tournament" I said, "We came here to win you your freedom."

"What are you talking about?" she asked.

"You have proven to me, others and yourself that you can win standing on your feet, but you need to feel that way about the things that make you uncomfortable as well. You need to learn to feel comfortable with feeling uncomfortable sometimes."

She proclaimed with even more determination, "No, I can't do this, you are asking me to do something I can't do!"

Here's what the final page I gave her said:

In your final match, you will immediately take your opponent to the ground. Stay on the ground and allow your opponent opportunities to try and attack you and submit you. You are not to attack them back but can try to get up as quickly as possible. You can defend yourself but DO NOT attack! Takedown and try to get up quickly and repeat. No attacking at all until I say you can.

Can you see why she felt the way she did?

With great hesitation, she climbed unto the combat stage and began the match. I must admit, there was a huge part of me that was just waiting for her to abandon the game plan and just use her sticks of dynamite.

Then it happened, she took her opponent down and stayed down for several seconds. When the opportunity to strike at her opponent presented itself, she did not attack. I saw that she was feeling uncomfortable. I saw doubt and fear sink in. I felt a desire to tell her right then and there to abandon the game plans final page and let the dynamite go off. I had to control myself and put my emotions in check and make sure I stuck to the game plan.

She finally got back to her feet only to take her opponent back to the ground. This time she was much faster getting back to her feet. I could tell that both competitors were already showing significant signs of fatigue. My student did it again and got the takedown, but this time found an opening for a submission and started to go for it. She looked over at me knowing that she had a very effective submission hold that would end the match and win her the tournament. I looked at her and shook my head. If looks could kill, that would have been my time to go.

Once she let go, the referee had the two competitors stand up and start the match again on their feet. This time the other girl took my student down and was very close to securing an armbar. I saw the immediate doubt, fear, panic and anxiety rush to my students face as she was now in a very uncomfortable position. She tried to roll out of the hold, but it made things worse. She hung in there and made several attempts to get free but was not successful.

The buzzer went off to signal the end of the first of two five-minute rounds. When she came over to me at our assigned corner for some water and rest, she did not say anything. I told her that things were going great and I was very proud of her. I then told her to stick to the game plan. No attacks — just go to the ground, defend yourself while getting back up as soon as you can.

Round two started with my student getting an immediate takedown and again sacrificing a few opportunities to strike and submit her opponent. At the three-minute mark of the final round, my student had been on the ground for over a minute. A this point she finally tapped out to a submission hold —that's it, she lost.

As soon as the ref separated the two competitors my student came running to me and excitedly gave me a big hug. She was so excited; we were both so excited. At one point during our celebration I looked over at the opponent's corner and they were staring at us with looks of confusion and faces that said, "Do you guys not realize that you lost?"

Did we lose? My student had to do something really hard for nearly ten minutes, but she did it and she was stronger for it. She explained to me that at some point in that second-round while on the ground she lost focus of her doubts and fears. She could tell those feelings were still there but because her focus was sticking to the plan, she felt freedom from not focusing on her doubts and fears.

This student went back to her regular teacher and Dojo and has since won many tournaments. When I see her around once in a while we start talking about that tournament as her greatest victory even though she technically lost. We were not at that tournament to win a trophy, and that's why we were so excited at the end of that last match. That day she won a match against fear and doubt.

The Spiritual

There is no doubt that for avid readers of the Book of Mormon, Nephi is a sure example of obedience, faith, diligence and sticking to a plan. In some of the final verses of 1 Nephi chapter 2 we see that Nephi prays to the Lord to know more about what his father had been taught and saw in a vision.

Nephi gains a knowledge for himself and is even praised by the Lord for his faith and diligence in seeking the Lord in humility (1 Nephi 2:19). Nephi is also told about many great blessings that will come into his life through his obedience to sticking to the Lord's game plan (keeping the commandments).

After this faith promoting experience, Nephi returns to the tent of his Father to rehearse to him what he has learned. As Lehi tells Nephi about the need to return to Jerusalem, Nephi gets to share with his father what he has learned when he declares:

"And it came to pass that I, Nephi, said unto my father: I will go and do the things which the Lord hath commanded, for I know that the Lord giveth no commandments unto the children of men, save he shall prepare a way for them that they may accomplish the thing which he commandeth them." (1 Nephi 3:7)

In the following verse, we see that Lehi completely understands that his son had an experience when we read, *"And it came to pass that when my father had heard these words he was exceedingly glad, for he knew that I had been blessed of the Lord." (1 Nephi 3:8)*

From many years of experience in practicing and teaching Ninjutsu I came to know that knowledge does not equal behavioral change. We can know something perfectly but still choose not to do anything about it. I think that's why I love these Nephi moments so much. Nephi has just discovered something about the Lord and himself and it's this new knowledge that led him to declare, "I will go and do."

The behavioral change for Nephi comes from his desire to go and do something about what he discovered. We value what we discover more than what we are told. So when Nephi declares, "I will go and do" he is really saying, "I will go and continue to discover." This commitment to keep discovering will lead to a changed heart and not just a changed opinion.

So, with one faithfully committed brother (Nephi), one willing brother (Sam) and two rebellious brothers (Laman and Lemuel) they set out to obtain the plates of brass. It's not very long after arriving in Jerusalem that Nephi's "go and do" declaration is put to the test.

Once they arrived in Jerusalem, they cast lots to see which lucky person would get to go in and ask Laban for the plates. The lot fell on Laman, who was not successful in acquiring the plates. In fact, he was thrown out and accused of being a robber and threatened with being killed (1 Nephi 3:13).

When Laman returned to his brothers and rehearsed this horrifying experience, he was "exceedingly sorrowful" and just wanted to go home (1 Nephi 3:14). Now Nephi would not have any of this "going home" nonsense for he had knowledge of the Lord and his heart was starting to change through these meaningful experiences. In 1 Nephi 3:15-16 we see him share his knowledge and understanding to his brothers and use very similar words when compared to 1 Nephi 3:7.

Now, we could jump all over Laman and Lemuel for their lack of faith, murmuring and zero desire to pray and seek God, but in this case and several other cases in the scriptures, they do demonstrate a desire to do good "that they might be faithful in keeping the commandments of God" (1 Nephi 3:21).

What Laman and Lemuel do next has always amazed and impressed me. They go back with Nephi and Sam to "gather together" their gold, and their silver and their precious things (1 Nephi 3:22). Can you see why this is impressive? These rebellious brothers loved their worldly possessions and lifestyle. This was not just their gold, silver and precious things, this was their inheritance that they are willing and ready to sacrifice. Go back now to Nephi's speech that motivated them and you will start to see that this was more than good thoughts that make sense. Nephi's words helped his brothers get past their sorrow of giving up their inheritance, only to hand it over for records that Laman and Lemuel seemed to never have cared about in the first place. These verses have taught me as much about Laman and Lemuel's desire to do good as about Nephi's courage and faith.

Unfortunately, when they returned, it did not go as well as they planned. Once Laban saw all of their worldly possessions, "he did lust after it" and thrust Nephi and his brothers out so he could take all their precious things for himself. To make sure they would not return or tell others what happened, he also sent his servants to kill them. (1 Nephi 3:25)

It's really important to note that as they run away and hide, Laman and Lemuel start to snap. They attack

Nephi and Sam by hitting them with a rod. I'm sure we have all had temper tantrums when our plans have not worked out the way we wanted them too. An angel appears to them and says some important stuff, but what really jumps out to me is when he says: "Behold ye shall go up to Jerusalem again, and the Lord will deliver Laban into your hands." (1 Nephi 3:29)

What happens next in 1 Nephi 3:31 demonstrates the powerful impact fear has on our minds and hearts. Before any words are spoken by any of the brothers, and just after the angel departs, Laman and Lemuel began to murmur at the thought of how powerful Laban is. What? Really! An angel just appeared to you and the very first thing that you decide to say is how powerful a mortal man is?

This seems so crazy when we read it, but this type of experience is more common than we care to admit. Despite having powerful, moving and spiritually uplifting experiences, we sometimes allow the fear of the moment to take our faith-promoting experiences hostage. From Laman and Lemuel we can see that fear truly blinds our minds and hardens our hearts from rejoicing in the moments where we have experienced divine intervention.

At this point, Nephi starts to sound like a broken record as he repeats to his brothers the same message he shared already, "let us go up again unto Jerusalem, and let us be faithful in keeping the commandments of the Lord" (1 Nephi 4:1).

After another rousing speech, his brothers take courage and head back to Jerusalem, again! This time Nephi takes action and heads into the city. As Nephi approaches the house of Laban, he sees that the Lord has delivered Laban into his hands.

Now, here is where I really learn a great lesson from Nephi. It's important to remember that Nephi's declaration, a declaration that has found its way into the hearts of Latter-Day Saints ever since March of 1830 (when the Book of Mormon was first printed) reminds us that the Lord will always prepare a way for us to accomplish the things that he commands us to do (1 Nephi 3:7).

Nephi knows the plan. The Lord spoke to Nephi and Nephi recently saw an angel that reaffirmed the plan and how the Lord will provide the way by placing Laban into his hands. With this knowledge, Nephi is now given another page in the game plan where he is asked to slay Laban (1 Nephi 4:10).

Well, Nephi knows what he has to do, after all he's taught his brothers (and us) a few times already in 1 Nephi 3:7 and verse 21 that we should be faithful in keeping the commandments of the Lord. Yet, Nephi doesn't declare "I will go and do" this time, does he? He says: "I shrunk and would that I might not slay him." (1 Nephi 4:10)

In other words, "I can't do this, this part of the game plan is too hard." It's in this very moment that I have learned more about Nephi and what real courage and faith look like. This moment where he briefly trades in the slogan, "I will go and do" and replaces it with a very temporary slogan, "this is too hard" is a game changer for me. There is a significant difference between theoretical faith of just knowing something, and applied faith that connects our hearts to understanding. What we see in these verses is Nephi leaving the realm of theoretical faith as he enters the reality of knowing by doing.

After a few spiritual promptings (1 Nephi 4:11-13) Nephi snaps out of his "this is too hard" slump and remembers what he knows (1 Nephi 4:14). His motivation increased in verses 15-16 in 1 Nephi 4 when he also realized that his people would not be able to keep the law of Moses without the law which happened to be on the plates he was trying to get.

After remembering what he already knew and feeling an increase in motivation to accomplish what the Lord has asked him, Nephi declares, "I did obey the voice of the Spirit."

Let's think back to that student that I trained. Think of all of her success in the tournament until I changed the game plan and she had to do something very hard. If I let her, she would have quit that final match and abandoned all her success that she had accomplished in the tournament up to that point.

If the spirit did not continue to prompt Nephi, would he have quit and gone home because that final attempt to get the plates was too hard? Would he have given up everything he had already done to get to that point because the last match was too hard?

I love the words from Elder Jefferey R. Holland: *"No matter what challenge you are currently facing, remember: "I did not come this far only to come this far." Keep going. Keep trying. Keep trusting. Keep believing. Keep growing. As I have said before, Heaven is cheering you on today, tomorrow and forever."*

We can continue to have meaningful spiritual experiences that remind us that the Lord will not ask us to do anything we can't handle. We will have moments that we will forget this principle of truth and feel overwhelmed by fear, anxiety and sorrow. In order to overcome these feelings, we need to remember that tough things are not a change in the game plan but are vital parts of the game plan, yes, they are the most important parts of the game plan.

Heavenly Father doesn't just decide one day to change everything just to mess us up. This life is by divine design and the plan of happiness can only truly be called that because we know that fear, anxiety and sorrow are parts of the plan as well.

We know what good feels like because we have experienced the bad. The bad moments do much more then help us know the good moments, they also provide us increased joy while in the good moments.

When I added the page to the student's game plan and she wanted to stop and quit, I was not changing the plan or even adding to it. I knew from the first time I met her what I was going to do. It was always part of the game plan though she didn't know that. I'm sure she wished she knew the whole plan ahead of time. I'm sure Nephi would have liked that as well at times, just as we do.

My student got back into the match because despite her fears, she trusted me as her teacher. Nephi finished what the Lord asked him to do because he trusted the Lord as his teacher. We need to trust the Lord as our teacher, who knows the game plan and will never ask us to do something we can't handle. The Lord sees much more than the big picture, he truly sees the whole picture. We need to have enough faith like my student and like Nephi to eliminate the question marks and replace them with exclamation marks.

NOTES

Final Thoughts

Throughout our lives we will have the opportunity to participate in many wonderful activities. We may play musical instruments, play sports, draw, paint, hike, fish, practice magic tricks, serve in callings at church and much more.

As we find joy in doing what we love I invite each of us to find Jesus Christ in all our activities — because he is there. I was touched when reading the account of the Savior's disciples in the book of Mark. After helping feed the five thousand they were asked to get into the ship and go to the other side to Bethsaida. (Mark 6:44-45)

The scriptures teach us that while they were on the ship the "wind was contrary unto them" which really means that the wind was making it difficult to get to where they needed to be. As the wind becomes increasingly challenging for these faithful rowers, Jesus walks out towards them on the sea. The part that is powerful to think about is when we know that Jesus Christ is out there with them, he loves them and will not leave them in their moment of challenge yet he "would have passed by them" if they did not call out (Mark 6:48-49).

How many experiences have we had in our lives where Jesus Christ is on the water with us, but we have not called out to him or recognized his presence? How often have we allowed him to pass by us when he was and is always willing and ready to come to us? Let's not let this happen. Let's make sure that no matter what we are doing, we are always doing it with Christ at the center.

We often do ourselves a significant disservice when we feel that Christ is too busy helping other people who are stuck in far more difficult "contrary winds." We may convince ourselves that Jesus Christ is too busy helping with major moments and does not have time for our minor moments. This is simply not true. Jesus Christ does not think about our moments as being major or minor, he's too busy loving us perfectly to care about the difference (D&C 38:7).

I filled out a survey once and was surprised to see Religion under the heading, "extracurricular." When we look at the definition of what extracurricular means, *"pursued in addition to the normal course of study"* we can see why I was taken back. Is our relationship with Jesus Christ in addition to our normal activities?

When we put Christ at the center of all we do, we can avoid ever checking the Religion box under extracurricular. When we make Christ the center of all we do we are also eliminating the potential hazards of doubt and fear (D&C 6:36).

Remember the definition of Spiritualjutsu is to use specific methods and techniques to develop the skills that will affect our spirits. Taking the time to ponder and reflect on my Ninjutsu experiences helped me identify valuable life lessons. Taking the time to ponder and reflect on these valuable life lessons helped me identify connections to the scripture stories I love. This method of pondering and reflecting led me to recognize that my personal experiences when connected to scriptural experiences were very similar. In 1 Nephi 19:23 we see Nephi practicing this when he taught, "for I did liken all scriptures unto us, that it might be for our profit and learning."

When I am practicing my Spiritualjutsu, I am likening the scriptures to my life through pondering and reflecting. I am not just reading the scriptures, I am responding to them.

Invitation to Practice

What is it you like doing? Once you are thinking about this activity you like doing, spend time pondering why you feel so good doing it. Now think about what you learned or are currently learning from doing your chosen activity. Can you make connections between your activity, how you feel and what you learned?

Doing this regularly with everything we do is the type of Spiritualjutsu practice that puts Christ at the center of all activities. This has been my method of increasing my spiritual capacity and has been another part of my spiritualjutsu.

Permanent

I once heard a senior Missionary ask someone, "practice makes what?" to which the person being asked responded, "perfect."

"No." said the missionary, "Practice makes permanent." I love that!

Bruce Lee said: *"Before I learned martial arts, a punch was just a punch and a kick was just a kick. When I studied martial arts, a punch was no longer just a punch and a kick was no longer just a kick. Now I understand martial arts, and a punch is just a punch and a kick is just a kick."*

Think about a time you decided to try something new. You probably realized fairly quickly that there is much more involved in learning this new thing then you first thought. It could be the piano, sports, drawing, acting or even cooking. My wife makes this amazing orange carrot soup and it never lasts long in our house once it's served. I learned recently that it takes her much longer to make that soup then I originally thought. The soup was no longer just soup, it meant more to me as I learned more about how much love and effort goes into the soup.

This helps us in recognizing the need to strengthen our relationship with Jesus Christ. The more we learn of him, the more we appreciate what he has done and trust what he has taught.

So, to make something permanently a part of us we need to practice, and through practice we discover the value of what we are doing. What happens when we practice being Christlike?

As we practice making Christ the center of what we do, He will become the best part of what we do. Our relationship with Jesus Christ will feel not only tangible and more fulfilling but it will also feel very familiar.

Conclusion

I have become great at Ninjutsu not because I was born this way or because I was blessed with great genetics. I am great at Ninjutsu because I practice all the time. The time we spend in practicing what we like doing will always increase our capacity to improve at it.

Do you think that Christ was able to perform all his mighty miracles just because he had divine genetics? Or was he able to perform those mighty miracles because every day he would focus and practice what he was taught from the Father? Each day, no matter how hard or difficult the temptations were, He kept practicing and discovering more about Himself and His Father which led to an increased understanding of us, His sons and daughters. We may often think that Christ came to know us personally through the giving of His life, but I have come to appreciate that He knows us intimately through the way He lived his life. I also know that because of His practice we have many permanents.

No matter what you enjoy doing, doing it with a Christ centered focused will magnify your love and appreciation for it. This is also true as we build relationships with others and learn to love and appreciate ourselves.

Jesus Christ doesn't just live; he lives for a purpose. You and I are that purpose. Practicing Spiritualjutsu really comes down to doing the things that strengthen our spiritual capacity to see Jesus Christ. I testify that as we practice Spiritualjutsu, we will come to rely on the teachings and atonement of Jesus Christ each day. As we rely on His teaching and atonement each day our skills to strengthen our spirits will increase and we will find meaningful and lasting joy.

x

Commonly Asked Questions

Now, as a real life, certified Ninja I have been asked many questions. Here are a few commonly asked questions I have been asked over the years. My answers to these questions are in ***bolded italics.***

Can you do the splits? ***Why would I ever want to do that to my legs?***

How hard can you really punch? ***I'm not sure, stay still and don't move…***

Do you jog for exercise? ***No. Ninjas hide in trees and take out joggers as they go by!***

Do Ninja's believe in God? ***The more important question is, DO YOU?***

I really like your Ninja boots, what kind of shoes do you normally wear? ***Sneakers!***

Tell me a Ninja joke…. ***Sure, but you'll never see it coming.***

How many push-ups can you do? ***All of them!***

Could you win in a fight against Chuck Norris? ***Yes. Wait… well maybe. Actually, in case he ever reads this – no!***

HOW ARE YOU GOING TO PRACTICE SPIRITUALJUTSU?

NOTES

NOTES

ABOUT THE AUTHOR

Mike Lafrance has black belts in Karate, Judo and Payton Ninjutsu. He has studied martial arts since he was 7 years old. In 2010 he founded his own Ninjutsu system called Kabutan Ninjutsu and continues to train thousands of students including several government agencies.

He joined The Church of Jesus Christ of Latter-Day Saints when he was 17 years old.

Mike was called to serve as a missionary and served in the Philippines Bacolod Mission. Now Mike works as a coordinator for seminary and institutes for the Church of Jesus Christ of Latter-Day Saints.

He lives in London Ontario, Canada. He is married to Crystal who he affectionally refers to as fancy face. Mike and Crystal have 3 amazing kids, Romeo, Neliah and Lowen.

Manufactured by Amazon.ca
Bolton, ON

35344935R00057